Invisible Illnesses and Emotions: Experienced by an Empath

AF623651

Robin Phillips

BookLeaf Publishing

Presentation by *BookLeaf Publishing*

Web: www.bookleafpub.com

E-mail: info@bookleafpub.com

ISBN: 978-93-95950-66-4

First edition 2022

DEDICATION

I have three dedications for this book.

The first is to my mom. You will never know how much you mean to me and how much you have helped me in this life. Watching you take charge, kick ass, and take names taught me how to live life. How you cared for us kids showed me how to love the life I live. I know we have had our differences (although we are pretty much the same person), but I know you have, and will continue to, love me through it all. You were my reason for living when I couldn't think of any others. You are the reason I am here to write this book. You will always be my reason. I love you. Thank you for everything you have done and everything you will ever do.

The second dedication is to all the people who fight their own minds and bodies every day. I know how alone you can feel and how hopeless situations can seem. You matter, even on the days when it feels like the opposite is true. I encourage you to fight. If this life will take you down anyway, fight like hell to enjoy every bit that you get.

The third is to the people who have fought this battle and lost. You are a warrior. I am so proud of you for fighting your fight for as long as you felt that you could. You fought hard and your effort was incredible. You will never be forgotten by the people who cared for you. You will live on in our hearts forever. We miss you.

ACKNOWLEDGEMENT

To all those who have played any role in my life, big or small, temporary or permanent, thank you for helping me become who I am today.

To those who made a positive impact, you mean the world to me. I wish I could name everyone I've known and what you mean to me.

I truly appreciate every effort you've made to support me and I will continue living my life until my body gives out.

PREFACE

As a person who has survived near death experiences, relationship violence, sexual abuse, car accidents, chronic pain, bullying, suicidal urges, and time itself, I must say that the hardest thing I have had to fight to survive is my own mind.

To those who fight, tooth and nail, to survive against themselves and the outside world every day, I commend you.

To those who don't have to fight their own minds and bodies every day, I hope you genuinely appreciate the hand you have been dealt.

No matter which category you fall under, this book is for you.
My hope is that these stories will make it easier for everyone to know what forms illnesses, emotions, and psychological conditions can take. We don't have to feel isolated and alone in our stories.
There is always someone who cares.

-National Suicide Prevention Helpline: 1 (800) 273-TALK

-National Domestic Violence Hotline: 1 (800) 799-SAFE or text "LOVEIS" to 22522

-Substance Abuse & Mental Health Services Helpline: 1 (800) 662-4357

-National Eating Disorder Helpline: 1 (800) 931-2237

-(RAINN) Rape Abuse and Incest National Network: 1 (800) 656-4673

-LGBT National Hotline: 1 (888) 843-4564

-The Trevor Project: 1 (866) 488-7386

-(NAMI) National Alliance on Mental Illness: 1 (800) 950-6264

The Effects of Insomnia

When insomnia invades your mind, it also invades your body. Restlessness, confusion, and headaches fill you with such a longing for sleep that anything seems to be a better alternative than being awake. Hit you with a two by four, anesthetize you, knock you out with a hammer, anything but being awake for more time when all you want to do is close your eyes and sleep.

When that feeling arises and sleep is the one thing that you cannot manage to do, the frustration sets in. It makes you feel empty and exhausted during the night and, without the reprieve that sleep provides, the next morning there is a bag of bricks on each shoulder and bags big enough for a week long trip under your eyes.

People hear insomnia and think 'trouble sleeping'. The silent parts range from anxiety to depression to lethargy that makes you feel lazy when you are just tired. Insomnia makes it feel like you can never be rested, never be fully awake, and never be completely whole. Insomnia takes a piece of you and removes it.

Insomnia will take your mind, spin it around until you are dizzy, then replace it only to have it be a pile of mush where a well oiled machine once sat.

The times when you find something to help you sleep, it seems like the greatest gift you could receive, until it isn't. Once the time comes for your alarm to go off, your body is so thankful for the sleep that everything in your body screams at you not to move for fear of waiting for the next peaceful round of sleep you may actually receive. Your eyes crack open, look at the enemy you've made of the clock, and wish you could turn back time and extend the only true sleep your mind and body have allowed you to have.

When you have reached the last possible moment before you are forced to move or be late, the anxiety sets in and you are forced to make quick decisions and quick actions to avoid the inevitability of the lack of sleep catching up to you. When it does, it is like it is chasing you at 120mph and no amount of swerving can keep you from experiencing the unpleasantness that is sleep deprivation. Your mind will melt, your temper will be short, and your energy level will be so low that you don't know how you managed to peel yourself off of the sheets that felt welcoming for the first time in weeks. You will find yourself losing focus, dropping things, and getting angry or exhausted by the smallest exchanges.

When insomnia rips sleep from you, it turns you into a roller coaster that you don't ever wish to ride. And when your mind finally gives you that reprieve to get lost in the sleep you have been longing for, you take it and don't look back. It won't stay for long. Enjoy it like a house guest. Your mind sure will.

The Fear of Rejection and Confrontation

She feared many things. Spiders, drowning, heights, but most of all, she feared rejection and confrontation.

Rejection scared her because she had been rejected, cast aside, and abused and she had come out of it alive, but not stronger. She came out the other side broken. She feared the people she cared about and connected to most would leave her and she would once again be alone in the world.

She feared confrontation for similar reasons. Her fight or flight response kicked in and she was ready to run in the other direction or kick someone's ass. Her trauma response was so used to being constantly barraged with new threats and perceived dangers that sometimes it went overboard during small confrontations. So she is ready to run or fight. Sometimes, neither of those are a good option. But they are the only ones that show up as options when her brain senses confrontations. She wants to stop running, but she just doesn't know how.

Hating the Skin You're In

She looked in the mirror and sighed. She should be used to disliking her reflection, but it still effected her with each glance. Made her feel gross, dumpy, and just plain ugly. Just as the words were thought, she sighed again. People always said not to be mean to herself. She just couldn't help it. Yes, she liked a few things about herself. Her color-shifting eyes and her copious tattoos. She disliked everything else.

She knew she should be nicer to herself, give herself compliments and positive words of affirmation, but she couldn't make herself be sincere. Try as she might, the sincerity never came. She was so tired of not being able to do the things that should make her feel better. She hated her appearance. She decided then to give herself a moment to be honest with herself. What didn't she like?

Everything but her eyes and tattoos. Her face was too long and her hair never cooperated, her stomach had an overhang, her muffin top and love handles seemed to taunt her, her breasts were sagging without the help of the children she could not have, and every part of her body screamed in agony at some point during the day until the moment she fell asleep. Not that she could do that correctly either.

She knew she could diet, work out, take supplements, do skin treatments, and do other things to fix herself, but it wouldn't change her opinion.

She knew because every time she did something different with her hair or changed her clothes, she would have that 'I actually look okay' moment, then the next time would make her sigh with the realization that her self love wasn't staying around, but fleeing from her like so many people had in her life.

She knew that she was supposed to love herself for who she was and how she looked. But in the moments when she looked at her reflection, she didn't know how it was possible to love someone like her. She had heard people say that no one will really love you until you love yourself, which worried her because she couldn't even stand to look at herself or hear her own laugh without immediately regretting the action because of insecurities and shame. She knew

that wasn't how it should be, but that's how it was. That's how she was.
She often hoped that she would wake up one day and love her reflection in the mirror, but that day never came. And because she was being honest with herself, she knew it never would. She knew that because she used to love who she was. When she was young, she had self confidence and self love. She had the willingness to see her beauty and know she was enough. But time and trauma change a person. People change people. And after hearing enough times that you weren't pretty enough and that you weren't going to be truly loved because you weren't what people were looking for, she started to believe it.

She went through trauma and abuse throughout her life until she got to a breaking point. And then she broke. Soon after, her spirit broke as well. She had dark moments, sitting in a closet, wishing her life would end, willing it to end. One day, she said enough. Enough of being who others thought she was. She got up, dusted herself off, and left the abuse behind.

She had started new since then, but trauma isn't something that can just be left behind. So she fought herself every day and year by year, she found out who she was and what she was capable of. She made goals and worked great jobs and made great friends. She had done it all on her way to taking her life back. But she could not genuinely enjoy her appearance. No matter who said she should and no matter how much she was supposed to, she just couldn't love the body she lived in.

When she had been honest with herself enough for the day, she shut all those peoples' voices and opinions in the small box that they were stored in and pushed it back down until she could almost forget it was there. She wouldn't let it control her life and after all, you don't need to love your appearance to enjoy your life. So she continued on as she always did, stopping to smell the roses and pretending to love herself in her entirety, just as she did every day of her life.

The Pain of Fear

She was scared. Every time he slammed a door or got frustrated, she trembled in her seat. She knew he wouldn't hurt her, but her body didn't listen to her logic. Her hands shook, her heart rate started to rise, she got sweaty, nervous, nauseous, and fight or flight kicked in. All she wanted to do in these moments was lock herself in a room or closet, far from the anger she could feel, as if it were a tangible thing she could touch.

Empathy could be good, but in these moments, it was not. She felt his anger and frustration and anxiety. All it did was heighten her own. She would unconsciously search for a reason to exit the area so the anxiety would not overtake her as it was him. She had dealt with that anger many times. Some were not as careful where they expelled it as he was.

He just slammed things and sighed and paced, which made her anxious enough, but others she knew had done so much worse. They had too much anger within them and they let it bottle up and form a hot ball of fire within them until they could no longer hold it in and they would let it explode from within them and char whoever was in its path. She was somehow always the one in its path.

She had to escape back then because when she didn't, they would hurt her. Sometimes it was the screaming and the saliva that would hit her face, making her jump when she was trying to hold her composure. She would try to look away, not just so she wouldn't see the fury in their eyes, but also because the heat and smell of their breath almost always made her eyes water and her stomach turn. And when they violated her, she played dead, dealt with the pain, and then cried herself to sleep.

The other people she had known were animals, deprived of any human decency or tact, just a shell of a person with a demon behind the disguise. She had absorbed the brunt of their fury for so many years, until she was freed by a guardian angel who she could never fully repay for the second chance at life.

She knew this person in front of her would not hurt her as the others had, but her subconscious didn't want to take any chances. So she would brace herself for every door slam; every heavy sigh and sideways look made her feel an inch shorter than she knew she was.

Sometimes she wished she could turn invisible so when he looked straight through her, at least there would be a reason. She wished that she could know exactly what he needed and exactly what to do to help him through the anxiety and frustration he was experiencing, but she had tried so many times. He never wanted her help. He just wanted to be angry. But she couldn't be around it without wanting to crawl out of her skin.

She often froze in those instances and held back the tears that came in the moments where neither fight nor flight were acceptable options. She knew the tears made her seem weak, but if only he knew why she cried. She didn't cry because she was sad in those moments. She cried out of frustration. The moments when she couldn't escape the anger and when fighting back would hurt more than help, the only thing left that would get rid of all of the pressure, adrenaline, and anxiety was her tears.

The anger pushed her to the precipice of the hill and when she looked from the drop back to the surge of anger and frustration that was pushing her over, she almost preferred to jump. To jump into the canyon of depression, anxiety, and tears was a far better option than getting covered and surrounded by the cloud of anger that seemed to be just barely hiding behind a mask of neutrality.

She could feel the anger rising, even if no one else around them saw it. She would not be charred by this person too. So she distanced herself when he was overtaken by rage. She often fought the urge to descend into a closet or room, lock the door and hug her knees to her chest. Instead, she put on music loud enough to disguise the sound of slamming cupboards and loud, heavy sighs, closed her eyes, and repeated to herself that she was okay and that he wouldn't hurt her like the former had. Her subconscious never seemed to believe her, but the repetition of the phrases always seemed to help her slip into a numb demeanor.

That's what she had taught herself to do in the bad moments. When the others would scream or slam things or hurt her, she would escape to the place she created where no pain could go. She ignored his actions and words and looks until she was so numb that her closest friend wouldn't recognize her. She had learned that in order to protect her spirit from being ground into the dirt and broken beyond repair, she would need to fold it up and force it into the deep recesses of her mind. It would be safe there. It always was.

With the others, she put it there so much that eventually, it refused to come back out. So that numb demeanor that was supposed to be only a safe place, a mask to wear to hide the pain, became the only version of her that she would allow to show. She was a shell of a person who could only show people the parts of her that she wasn't afraid to lose. She took her heart off of her sleeve and built an impenetrable wall around it that would keep even the toughest warriors at bay.

When the others weren't a problem anymore, she attempted to open the lock on the wall, but in all the commotion and pain, she found that she had lost the key. The heart and personality she had locked away so long before were stuck, as if on strike from being denied for so many years. For years after, she had to chip at the wall and tear it apart, brick by brick, to gain access to who she was. But every brick removed just showed her another part of her old self that she couldn't accept back in.

Every time the anger started, she could feel her progress and her confidence crawl over the wall she had built long ago. So she put all of the bricks back into place and locked it up tight so that who she was now wouldn't crawl into the abyss. She would not welcome that numbness into her life again. Even on the angry days, even when things were slammed and sighs were had and voices were raised, she would rather fight than let herself slip away again. When fleeing was required, she would do so. But until that moment, she would fight for herself and her right to be exactly the person that she had fought herself and everyone else to become. No one was taking that away now.

Invisibility In Real Life

When she was a child and people would ask what her favorite super power was, she would answer confidently, "Invisibility!". When she was young, she would've done anything to have that superpower. As she grew older, it seemed more and more far fetched with each passing year. And then she got to the age where she realized that she got that superpower she wanted, but not in the way that she had hoped.

To some people, she was, indeed, invisible. She didn't get to choose who saw her or if anyone did at all, but she was invisible often without even realizing it. In line at the grocery store when people walked into her like she wasn't even there, or when someone had a conversation seemingly through her head to the person on her other side until she got uncomfortable enough to leave her seat as to not be talked at (or through?) for the entire evening.

Invisibility was happening, even then, as she tried having a conversation with him and he looked straight through her, never making eye contact. Taking the notes of a drama teacher he never had to look over the audience's heads instead of looking at them; it helps with stage fright. Except in his case, when looking over his audience's head frustrates her and makes her feel invisible to him. Like she doesn't exist in his world.

That feeling was the part of invisibility she didn't expect. The feeling of being completely and utterly alone because everyone she tried to speak to just stared through her, as if her forehead had a window into all of life's answers whenever she opened her mouth. She decided then and there that she didn't want her superpower anymore. She no longer wanted to be looked through, run into, and talked at like she wasn't there.

The bad part was though, she didn't know how to give her superpower back. She tried offering it back to the universe politely, like exchanging a Christmas sweater that is ugly and three sizes too big. When that didn't work, she made the universe some pretty big promises if it would just let her be seen again. On and on she went, trying to figure out how to take off her finicky invisibility cloak. She tried many things to get him to see her instead of being the window through which he could watch the television.

At one point, she stopped trying to be visible all together. She let herself sink into the background, like the backup dancer that no one is ever really watching. After a while, she realized that being seen seemed worth fighting for, so she got up off of the couch, walked over to him, and spoke over the television. She told him that she was tired of being invisible to him and that she wasn't allowing to happen any more. As she spoke, she felt the invisibility cloak lift off of her gently, one centimeter at a time, as he looked at her instead of through her for the first time in months.

It was short-lived, as are most good things, and he soon went back to being distant and moody, but for the first time, she realized how to take off the invisibility cloak for good. She wasn't just going to lose the knack for invisibility by doing nothing.

To lose the uninvited superpower, she had to make herself seen. She had to push past the invisibility and shove her way into the light if she had any hope of controlling this power she received. Each time she pushed into the light, she felt the cloak loosen a bit more until she felt as though she wore a light scarf instead. Once she had that scarf in her hands, she smiled. No one could stop her now.

Living as Another

She sat with her back to the room, hearing them laugh, no ability to make it stop. As she tried to make the fresh batch of tears absorb back into her tear ducts, one slips and ruins all her effort. They were cruel, but a small part of her felt that she deserved it. She didn't, but she felt that she did. Self-esteem was a skill that was always lost to her. She didn't like herself, so how was anyone else supposed to like her. She knew they did, but didn't understand how.

As she sat and faced the wall, she wondered why everyone else got to love themselves and she didn't. Why did everyone get to love how they looked and who they were while she sat in silence, contemplating the things she hated most about her lonesome self. She liked her skills, but the beauty of her physicality and personality were lost on her that day, as they always were. She tried to think of what she genuinely liked about herself.

She could come up with only two things. The tattoos she had acquired over the years and her unique color shifting eyes. Not many people knew of her eyes though, as almost no one bothered to look into them. To see the pain and anxiety that lie there. To see the person inside crying out for help, not that anyone ever looked close enough to notice. When she was young, she was told that crying in front of people was a weakness and you had to be strong. Always had to be strong in front of others. So she pushed down the tears and saved them for later. She would open that floodgate when she was alone. As she always did.

She wasn't raised to be soft, but hard as stone. At least, in appearance. She was not hard as stone as so many wanted her to be. All she wanted was to be able to show who she was to the people around her. She was so scared that her weakness would drive them away. So she showed no one. She showed them the side of her that everyone liked. The confident, kind, excitable person she had concocted to put others at ease. They loved that version of her. But when she would start to let them in, bring down that side and show them who she was underneath, they never liked it quite like her mask. So she kept her mask on. Only taking it off in the solace of nighttime or in the moments when she was alone. That's the way it needed to be, so that's the way it was. They'd never see her for who she was because her weakness was too big of a flaw for anyone to handle. That's just the way it had to be.

The Pain of the Sunrise

She woke up in her bed and cursed the day for coming and the sun for rising yet again. If only perpetual night could fall so she wouldn't have to rise with the sun. It wasn't the rising itself that was the problem. It was the pain. It rocked her to her core and made her dizzy at its strength.

The pain decided what she could do and when, grabbing hold of her spine and tugging on it, harder and harder at a dizzying frequency, as if plucking on harp strings made of steel. It grabbed and tugged until she felt as if her spine would pull through the skin of her back and separate completely from her body.

When the pain went to her shoulders, it felt like there was a space inside her joints that just wouldn't go away; pressure and pain intermingled into the perfect irritating pair, waiting to ruin any activity that requires them to do anything over her head. When it moved to her knees, they too had pressure, but sometimes it became too much and her knee would burst out of its socket like a geyser, effectively erasing any feeling she had in her leg and replacing it with nothing.

All of the different pains were bad on their own, but she dealt with them all, every day of her life. Some days, finding the will to live was harder than facing the physical pain she knew she would endure. But rise she did. Every day without fail. Once she was out of her bed, the pain started creeping in. Her neck felt stiff as a board and her shoulders felt like she had been laying bricks in her sleep. But she trudged on and started her day.

She went to work, turning on the seat warmer in her car on a 60^0 day so that the heat would help loosen up the muscles in her already too tight back. As she sat outside her workplace with her seat warmer on high, she begrudgingly left the relative comfort of her warm seat to walk inside of her workplace and begin the day. As she passed the bush of marigold flowers that stood tall against the great height of the building, she paused long enough to inhale the bright fragrance and give herself the final push she needed to walk through the door.

Throughout the day, there would be pain, pressure, and anxiety, but she would make it through. She always did. When she got home, she would take a long, hot shower and lay on a heating pad until her back muscles ceased to tremble and spasm. The relief was comforting, if only for the short period it lasted. As she lay down to sleep, she knew it would evade her as it always did.

She began to make up stories in her head about lives where she didn't have pain, where she was heard, where she could be fixed. Finally free from the bindings of this constant barrage of pain that held her to the earth's crust, never letting her rise to the level she aspired to be at. Her pain inspired fear and trepidation. She didn't have control over her own body and it drove her insane.

Slowly, she imagined just driving off a cliff, crashing into a guardrail on the highway, carbon monoxide poisoning, or just simply not eating until her already-too-low blood sugar plummeted and sent her into the sleep filled abandon that is hypoglycemic shock. Whatever the way, it always sounded appealing, compared to the alternative. The pain that lasted hours and days at a time being the only guaranteed constant for the rest of your life.

She wondered if people knew how that felt. Not the actual pain, because she wouldn't wish that on others, but the emotions behind being put off by every doctor and nurse she saw and being told that it was growing pains (at 24 years old), pulled a muscle (the same muscle for the last 14 years?), and so many other excuses. That's all they were. Hollow excuses for the girl they all thought was faking it.

They all thought it was a show, all for attention. "You're too young to have back problems.", they all said. Too young? It wasn't her decision to be in constant agony. She knew she was too young for it, but it was there. It was happening. It was real and no one cared enough to believe her. To really listen at all. She was dismissed and waved on. Off to the world that was full to the brim with the things that caused her the most pain.

Existing caused her pain on its own, without other people or any activities to make it begin each day. Every morning, she opened her eyes and willed today to be the day the pain isn't there when she rises. But every day, it reappears just as it was the day before. And it all begins again.

Holding Back the Flood of Rage

Anger is a beast of its own kind. It doesn't have a conscience or guilt. It just has all the time in the world to make your day go spinning out of control like a car on black ice. Spinning and twirling until you are dizzy, anxious, and so nauseous that it is hard to breath. It makes you want to dig your feet in and argue, battle, fight, win!

What it doesn't do is help. It doesn't help with friendships, relationships, or partnerships. It is a hindrance that all with emotions feel. It hinders your ability to be rational, to see the other point of view, to have a logical conversation about your thoughts, and to hold yourself back so you don't say the things you keep inside.

Holding back anger is difficult, but holding back the uncompromising feeling of wrapping your fingers around someone's throat until you see the life slip out of their eyes is even harder. To convince yourself that this person shouldn't be killed when they don't even deserve to breathe.

Anger makes you want revenge and justice and change! It can make you want to shout from the rooftops, but it can also make you want to hide away from the world for fear of hurting someone too badly to take back. Never being able to truly be who you are and express what you feel because it is too dangerous for those around you. Anger can make you stop on a dime or plan revenge for months.

Anger can do so many things and take so many forms. The thing that determines what anger WILL do, is you. You are the floodgates and the walls and the guards. You are the army that is dedicated to keeping that flood inside. Putting your sanity and your morality on the line to keep the harsh waters at bay, for fear of drowning anyone who is in the basin below.

You are always on guard, always in check, and always ready to fight or flee. Fight to keep those gates closed and flee when you are unsuccessful and the rage pours out in waves. When the rage gushes out of the cracks in the wall and you try so hard to simultaneously patch the leaks and keep the rest standing, you know in reality, that it will break. So you run.

You take all of the water you are holding behind that wall you built and you run as far and as fast as you can until you are at another basin that houses only you. Because if anyone is going to drown in this pool of anger, it will always be you. Who else will bear this anguish? Who else will wear your battle scars? You are the person who keeps the water at bay and you are the only person who is guaranteed to get crushed when the wall breaks.

So why do we wall up all of this water and anger and hurt and let it fall down on us later? Why do we hold in everything we are angry about and let it destroy the person we are inside? Why do we let the anger control us instead of us controlling it?

Anger is that wave, that basin, and that beast. It is whatever it wants to be. The only things that we can do are decide how long we will keep the wall up to hold the water in and who we will let it crush when it falls.

The Stages of Grief

Grief is a powerful feeling. Only matched by anger in its strength.

It ebbs and flows like the ocean; constantly pushing and pulling your emotions around until you are at the mercy of the sea.

No control over when or where it will hit you next. In the supermarket, the bank, at your friend's house, or on the highway heading to your next destination.

Grief will hit you whenever or wherever it wants to, like a sucker punch to the gut. It makes you sad, angry, shaky, and lonely.
It will pluck at your heartstrings like a harp until you are crying into your steering wheel at a red light.

Your world will be turned upside down until you don't know how you ended up in a hole you didn't dig.

Grief will make you question everything, and it will gain you a new perspective. Maybe that's what grief is. The waves you ride to get yourself over and through losing someone or something important to you.

The process in which you learn the hard lessons that you never wanted to learn. The lessons and moments that take you to where you don't want to be and make you think about things you would rather not think about.

Grief teaches you about yourself and it is important to learn those lessons.

Because only in working through our grief, do we grow and learn to appreciate life as it was.

Then we move on to life as it is now.

The Promise of Death and the Feelings of Life

Broken. Alone. Afraid.

That's how she felt every day of her life. Scared to start the day and ready to end it before it began. When she woke up in the morning and looked outside, all she saw was a bright sun and a lonely world.

Is this what it was like for everyone? Did everyone feel broken, alone, and afraid? Was that all thauld be? Just an endless torrent of sadness, pain, and waiting until it ends.

Maybe that's why no one knows the secret to life. Because the only secret is that everyone feels eternally anxious and uncomfortable.
Why does it have to be this way? Why can't we live in a world that doesn't make people feel how she feels every day when she wakes up.

People keep saying. "Whatever doesn't kill you, makes you stronger.". What if it doesn't? What if this world breaks you down and tears you up inside, just to make you easier to swallow when the end comes?

And come it will. When it does, she will go out the way she came in.

Scared, alone, confused, and ready.

Accepting Death

Sunshine, a warm pool, and family made her day great. One member would make it life changing, and another would save the life that had changed.

Playing with the little ones, atop large inflated sea creatures. They were young and delighted. She was playing with them and an older brother. Splashing, pushing the littles around, laughing. A normal day that turned not so normal very quickly.

He came outside and entered the pool. He tried to get involved in playing with the littles, but they were preoccupied playing with her. That's all the reason his brain needed; an excuse to snap from decent stepbrother to a blank, cold stare that would make your skin crawl. She knew that stare well and she knew it came with consequences. She had learned that already. Only this time, she didn't see the stare.

As she played with the littles, he snapped into a cold, harsh version of himself and decided that she deserved to pay for taking the attention away from him with the littles. The price he wanted, he decided her life would suffice.

He grabbed her by the shoulders when she was alone for a moment and shoved her under the water. She didn't panic at first because siblings dunk each other. She assumed he would let go in a moment. Except he didn't. So she thought he was just taking a bit longer than he should. As she waited, something in her brain clicked. He wasn't letting her up because he didn't plan to. That realization hit and she knew she had to fight. She did all she could under water. Hitting his legs and any other body part she could reach, trying to push against his hands towards the surface, trying to get away in whatever way she could. Then another thought clicked in, even harder to except than the last. Her fighting wasn't working and it wasn't going to. She realized that he wasn't going to let go and she couldn't get away. She couldn't save herself. Then she just thought, "I'm going to die down here." She knew, in that moment, that her time was up. So she stopped fighting. She let the pressure of his hands hold her down as her lungs felt hot, tingly, and like they could explode any moment. As her lungs filled with the most unbearable pain, she started to feel dizzy.

Just as she started to drift toward unconsciousness, the weight on her shoulders was suddenly lifted. She paused for a moment because she almost didn't believe it. She dove towards the surface, coughing, gasping for air, holding herself up by the side of the pool.

While she was shocked back into the land of the living, her stepbrother decided that the penalty for interfering with drowning her was a chokehold for the brother. He tried to get him off and ended up having to punch him in the mouth to get him to let go. She rushed to get the littles out of the pool and sent them inside. She and the older brother got out of the pool and left him in it, spitting blood into the pool as it drained from his face. As she walked away from the pool, everything that had just happened was swirling through her head. Just after she accepted that she wouldn't make it out of the pool alive, she was saved. She was grateful every day that the older brother saved her life.

A lot of realizations, lessons, and phobias resulted from her experiences that day. It caused her fear of drowning, which then led into just a general fear of water. That developed into fear of deep, dark bodies of water because of what lies underneath. She had a hard time even showering. Couldn't watch any movie with water scenes without that sense of sheer panic starting to set in. She didn't know about any of that yet. All she knew is that she was alive and for that, she would always thank her brother. She would learn the realities of trauma later.

I Would Like To Die, I Think.

I would like to die, I think.

Not because of the manner of death as much as the freed soul I would be after.
Done with my mortal toil, done paying dues that I don't believe I owe. Done with the material and monetary worries of the world.

Yes, I think I would like to die.
My death doesn't have to be glorious, brave, big, or mighty. It just has to arrive at some point. To free me from the pain and agony of another waking day. Opening my eyes to the still too-dark skies, throwing back the covers sheathed in cat hair and padding through the pitch dark room, trying not to wake the other inhabitant of our bed as I blindly search for the clothes I laid out the night before. Every day started like this. Not wanting to get up and face the day, but rather crawl back under the covers and sleep the day away, just on the off chance I won't wake up this time. But I do, every time.

People say that I am too negative, I'm a pessimist, I'm too dark, and maybe I am all of those things. But I see myself as a realist. I look at what I've been dealt and I deal with it however I can. I expect things to go wrong in my life because they usually do, and if they don't one day, I get to be pleasantly surprised. Not that those random surprises are worth the daily mortal toil, but still. It is a burst of sunshine on an otherwise cloudy day.

Yes, I think dying sounds okay.
When I say I would like to die, I may not mean what you think. You see, I used to be suicidal. You would've been too if you were in my shoes at that time. I came close once to ending everything, but I couldn't pull the trigger. I knew the people I would hurt if I did. Permanent solution to a temporary problem, they say. They are technically right. Sometimes, the problem isn't temporary though. Sometimes the almost constant ache in your bones is too much to bear and it makes you want to tear your skin off in agony.

The burning ache grows stronger with each passing moment until it feels as though your spine will be ripped from your body in the least convenient route. That pain isn't temporary for me. If it isn't my spine, it is my ankle, knee, shoulders, reproductive system, head, or some other part of my body that decides to take its turn. So yeah, I'm okay with dying. Not feeling that pain anymore, every waking day? Sounds great.

The problem is, I can't remove myself from this earth. Believe me, I've tried. I couldn't pull the trigger. I wanted out so badly, but I knew the type of pain that would cause my family. So I couldn't pull the trigger. Since then, I've made a promise that when I leave this earth, it won't be from my own hands. That promise is the only thing that holds me to this ground and keeps me alive some days. Most important one I've ever made.

Dying sounds okay to me. I wish I could pick my manner of death though. I don't want to drown or burn alive. If I could choose, I would die in my sleep. But, then again, wouldn't everyone? It isn't the fantasy deaths I used to imagine when I was actively suicidal, but it is better than car accidents and dying on impact paround.

So yeah, dying sounds okay.
Just peacefully please?

The Realities of Suicidal Thoughts

"Are you sure you're safe? Suicidal thoughts aren't normal."

I appreciate you checking. I really do. But this is why I don't tell people when I feel like that. Because everyone assumes that when I'm thinking like that, I'm going to act on it. Which I won't. Not just because I made a promise, but because I know how many people I would hurt in the process. I promised that when I leave this world, it won't be from my own actions.

I never promised that I wouldn't think about it or talk about it. Because it is a thought process that is around a lot. I would be surprised if it isn't in almost everyone with chronic pain. That doesn't mean I'm going to hurt myself and it doesn't mean that I am not thankful for the days when I don't feel this way.

But some days I do. More days than not, some weeks. There is a lot in my life that I have to recover from. I am still recovering, every day. Recovery of any kind comes with backsliding and grief and anger and immense sadness. And sometimes, suicidal thoughts. As long as the backsliding stops and the progress continues, the other things are side effects of learning how to live your life in recovery from your life.

I'm not actively suicidal, nor will I let myself be again in my life. But passive suicidal tendencies help remind me that I am human, mortal, and fallible.
And that's okay.

Stand and Fall

She stood up and immediately sat back down, the swaying in her head reminding her that she can't just get up.

She had to go from laying down to sitting up to standing, but she had to take breaks in between. Not because of the pain, present as it was, but because the dizziness was a warning sign of the fall that would come if she didn't listen to her body. She should be used to the frequent pauses in motion after the slightest change in position, but she hated that her body had more control of her actions than she did. She hated being out of control, but her body had final word, as always. End of conversation.

Forgiving the (Seemingly) Unforgivable

He had done so many things wrong. The broken promises, the phone calls to ask about presents that never came, cards that never got sent, return calls that never happened when he said they would. Always a few months later, she would get a call filed with apologies and promises of "making it up to her". Making it up is right. She decided one day that she was done. As she cried on that day, she swore that she would never let him make her feel this way again.

She tried to ignore him for the most part, which wasn't hard because he barely ever made any contact. She went through her school years and young adulthood wondering why he did so many things. She never considered forgiving him. She held onto that anger until she couldn't anymore.

Then she let go. She let go of the anger and who he used to be. She didn't want any part of who he was now, but she was glad he had changed for the better. She finally forgave the person she never thought she could forgive. All the more easy to forget and move on. That she did. Now he was little more than a stranger.

The Pain Behind PCOS

She grabbed the last of the pizzas to put in the oven and slid them in just as she doubled over in pain.

'Not this again', she thought as she clutched her abdomen as if to tear out the parts of her that were causing so much anguish. She glanced around at the empty restaurant and was thankful for the temporary reprieve from one of her challenges.

She leaned against the counter and took deep breaths, willing the pain to leave her alone, but knowing it would likely take hours to fade into a dull ache. She grumbled under her breath and cursed the genes that made her female. Being in pain is never fun, but being in pain from parts that will never be used is horrible. She didn't want children, so why did her reproductive system scream so loudly?

Her body was so angry at her barren uterus that her ovaries decided to create pipe bombs instead of eggs. They would get to the end of their individual timers and BOOM! The bomb goes off and delivers on its explosive nature. The force of the rupture makes her feel like a red hot ice pick to the pelvis.

Her vision wavers, eyes fill with tears, her abdomen aches with the free fluid, once contained in the biological pipe bomb called a cyst, that now sloshes around, waiting to be re-absorbed. She leans on the counter more, taking some weight off of her shaky legs, and blinks back the tears that threaten to tell her secrets.

As much as she wanted to slip into a booth and cry until the pain subsided, she knew that wasn't an option. Not only because she had a restaurant to run, but also because she knew it wouldn't help. The pain would be there, nagging at her, stabbing and prodding at the most sensitive parts of her either way. If the pain will be there regardless, why not work through it? At least, that's what she had learned since the pain started. She had been experiencing those pipe bomb pains for years and she had tried every response. This is what worked for her.

She took a few more deep, steadying breaths and pushed herself up off of the counter. She gasped at the pain ricocheting through her abdomen and groin and pushed through it. Realizing that the pizzas were done, she picked up the pizza paddle and started pulling them out. She was trying her best to ignore the waves of pain crashing into her, ever-present and unforgiving. She crossed her fingers and hoped for a short storm.

I Am Me

Does anyone care?
Am I alone?
Am I talking to you... or to myself? Is there someone there? Someone that can help me? Am I lost or just losing? Am I gone or just starting to go? When will I see you or have I already seen you? When will I meet you or have we already met? Is anyone out there?
Anyone who cares?
Anyone at all?
Anyone?
Hello?
Am I really on my own?

No matter how many questions I ask, no one answers. No matter how many jokes I tell, no one laughs. No matter how long I stand there, no one acknowledges my presence. I have so many questions; I need so many answers. And yet... no one is there to answer my questions or ask any of their own.

Am I invisible or merely ignored?
Am I taken or left?
Good or bad?

Am I loved? Do I even know what love is?
Do I want a friend or do I want an acquaintance?
Who am I?
A loser? A follower? A leader? A joker? A speck? A friend? A smile? A thought in the dark? A wanderer? Am I patient soul? A confused child? An unwanted visitor? An uninvited guest?

Am I sane or insane? Cold or warm? Yes or no? Here or there? Child or adult? Nomad or settler? Lady or maid? Invisible or seen? Heard or ignored? Stopped at or passed by? Loved or exiled? Hated or revered?

Wanted... or just pushed to the side like an unwanted gift. Left. Sitting alone. Being alone.

Is that really what is expected of me?
To just sit here and be ignored and shoved aside? To be left to find my own way? Or am I expected to learn? To rise? The question here is... why am I put through all of this. The answer? Who knows. My answer?

I believe that I was pushed down, so I could learn to rise up. I was ignored so I could learn to make myself heard. I was left so I could find my own path. The way I was supposed to go. The way that will lead me to my future. I believe that I wandered so I could find where I truly belong. I was left and pushed and shoved, but I now see why.

I was treated like a no one so that I could finally realize that I am so much more than that. So much more than what teachers, parents, kids, students, and other people say.

I am me. I am myself. I am loved and trusted and needed. I am my own savior. My own boss. My own servant. My own person. I now know that all of the hardships, pain, suffering, and hate was to make me realize that I am so much more.

That I am the amazing, talented, beautiful person that I was always meant to be.

I am Me.

Misery Loves Company

Whatever life brings you, you must try to be stronger than it. I can tell you right now, you need to persevere because if you don't, it becomes a long, drawn out band of misery. The kind of misery that invades your every sleeping and waking thought. The kind that will haunt you no matter what you are doing or what you are thinking about.

It takes up your mind and your thoughts and it will keep you awake at night with thoughts of what if. When you get into that kind of misery, you need to be aware that it is not a good place to be. You need to turn and run in the opposite direction as fast as your legs can carry you. Run to the security that is a restful night's sleep without having to worry about the depression that would follow otherwise. In times of crisis, your mind revers to the fight or flight reflex and, at times, it is not the best way to go. But in these instances, where survival is imminent and requires work, it is essential to human survival to be very sure of your choice.

That choice depends on how your mind is working. If it is working well, you will choose to run from the depression, hurt, and worry. But if your mind isn't enjoying the experience of decision making, you may choose to stay at your present location. In which case, it isn't anything someone else can change. Eventually, I hope you run.

In My Life

In my life, I've been through so many heartaches. Love isn't easy, but it shouldn't be this hard. Time flies when you're having fun, but it slows way down on the off times and it is times like those when you learn to appreciate the good times.

When life slows down, take a deep breath, relax as much as you can, and think about what has happened, but more importantly, what is to come. If you only focus on the past, it will tear you down. But you should never forget the past. The past is what made you who you are, good or bad. They all affected you in some way and no matter what they did, it brought you along farther into life than you were before. Difficulties help as well as good things.

Time teaches us that no one is perfect and if we accept that, it makes us much better at opening our minds and our hearts to love and hate. If you only open up to one, you will only see one side of the world. For some people, that is perfection in itself because some like to only see the right or the wrong. The best way to see life is straight on, full force. Life is full of surprises, but you will miss all of them up you don't let yourself open up and let them in.

If you have a certain opinion on something and are set in your ways, that is fine. But if you aren't quite set in your ways about it, open your mind. Hear all sides. Be open to new experiences and explanations. Some things, I wouldn't want to compromise on either. But that doesn't mean that I won't listen and try to understand the other person's point of view. Life is full of biases and opinionated people. Just because their sides and points are different, doesn't mean they aren't worth a listen. You never know. Maybe someday, your opinion will change. It will never change though, if you never listen. People have the right to their opinions. They have the right to express themselves. That doesn't mean you need to believe them. It doesn't necessarily mean that you should shut them out either. You decide.

A Tear

A tear falls down and hits the ground. I don't know why he hates me. He's made me cry more than one time and yet he turns away, more than once in a while.

People have told me, they're only tears. It doesn't matter as long as you're here. They just don't get it. They never will. I don't regret it, I never will. It makes me sad, sometimes I'm lonely. But what's really bad is that I'm the only person who sees and believes me.

I've cried my eyes out, looking for a way. A means of escaping another dreary day. What really matters us the wait that lies in store. I'll have to get through it if I want to be something more.

I am worth something, that much I know. You may not believe me, but I tell you so. My heart has been broken and I know it's true. But now I am hoping, I can keep it safe from you.

I don't wear my heart on my sleeve. I used to trust, used to believe. That my heart would be safe there, safe from any harm. I know better now. Excuse me. I'm going to write you a letter now.

"Dear loving father, you've made my tears. You can't tell me and make me believe that you aren't the source of my crying. I know it for a fact and I can't hide it anymore. You broke my heart and it's still sore. You ripped away my trust like the pages of a book. Now you know I must restore the stuff you took. So listen up. You took my trust away. So listen up. That ends today."

How to Prevent a Collapse of Self

She looked at the clock and realized she had been coloring for hours and it was now dark outside. She smiled and put her coloring stuff away near the other supplies she had for her copious hobbies. People always asked why she had so many hobbies.

Why are you so busy all the time? Why don't you give yourself some down time? What they didn't understand is that busy was her down time. Her mind needed to stay occupied or it found ways to be occupied. And because an unoccupied mind usually led to intrusive thoughts, suicidal ideations, and other unhealthy things, she preferred busy to not.

Why shouldn't she? The perfect way to occupy your mind is with something creative that requires a smattering of critical thinking. She had all the hobbies she could muster and gave herself bonus points for the hobbies that help others as well. She appreciated everyone's concern and knew they all meant the best, but being busy isn't a bad thing when you would be doing worse otherwise.

www.ingramcontent.com/pod-product-compliance
Lightning Source LLC
Chambersburg PA
CBHW051735130826
49812CB00033B/870
9789395950664